MW00694521

The Doctrine & Covenants
PUZZLE BOOK

The Doctrine & Covenants
PUZZLE BOOK

KIMIKO CHRISTENSEN HAMMARI

CFI
Springville, Utah

© 2008 Kimiko Christensen Hammari

All rights reserved.

No part of this book may be reproduced in any form whatsoever, whether by graphic, visual, electronic, film, microfilm, tape recording, or any other means, without prior written permission of the publisher, except in the case of brief passages embodied in critical reviews and articles.

This is not an official publication of The Church of Jesus Christ of Latter-day Saints. The opinions and views expressed herein belong solely to the author and do not necessarily represent the opinions or views of Cedar Fort, Inc. Permission for the use of sources, graphics, and photos is also solely the responsibility of the author.

ISBN 13: 978-1-59955-191-3

Published by CFI, an imprint of Cedar Fort, Inc., 2373 W. 700 S., Springville, UT 84663
Distributed by Cedar Fort, Inc., www.cedarfort.com

Cover design by Nicole Williams
Cover design © 2008 by Lyle Mortimer
Edited by Allison M. Kartchner

Printed in the United States of America

10 9 8 7 6 5 4 3 2 1

Printed on acid-free paper

contents

joseph smith and the doctrine and covenants

crossword puzzle

JOSEPH SMITH

ACROSS

3. Joseph had an operation on his ____.
6. Joseph's age when he prayed to know which church to join.
8. His father's name (3 words)
12. Where the Smith family lived at the time of the First Vision
14. The Sacred _____
15. Angel who appeared to Joseph
16. Joseph saw two _____ directly above his head.

DOWN

1. Month Joseph was born
2. State where Joseph was born
4. Joseph was told to join ____ of the churches.
5. Book in the Bible that helped Joseph
7. Joseph wanted to know which _____ was true.
9. His wife's name (2 words)
10. Joseph prayed in the ____ of 1820.
11. His age when he had his operation
13. Month in which the Church was restored

Solution on page 80.

3

crossword puzzle

D&C 135:3

Complete the crossword puzzle to the right by filling in the missing words from the verses below. For example, 2A in the verse below is the missing word that goes in 2 across, 21D is 21 down, and so forth.

3 Joseph Smith, the (11D) and Seer of the Lord, has done more, save (10D) only, for the (13A) of men in this world, than any other man that ever lived in it. In the short space of (16A) years, he has brought forth the Book of Mormon, which he translated by the gift and power of (12D), and has been the means of publishing it on two (1D); has sent the fulness of the (9D) gospel, which it contained, to the four quarters of the (5A); has brought forth the revelations and (4A) which compose this book of Doctrine and Covenants, and many other wise documents and instructions for the benefit of the children of men; gathered many (18A) of the Latter-day Saints, founded a great (15A), and left a fame and name that cannot be (8A). He lived (12A), and he died great in the eyes of (17D) and his people; and like most of the Lord's (2A) in ancient times, has (3D) his mission and his works with his own (6A); and so has his brother (14D). In life they were not (7D), and in death they were not separated!

Solution on page 80.

5

word search

D&C THEMES

Below is a list of some of the themes in the Doctrine and Covenants. Search for them in the word search on the following page (don't search for words in parentheses). Then place the remaining letters in the grid, from left to right, in the spaces at the bottom of the page to reveal a hidden message.

BAPTISM

BUILDING ZION

(CHURCH) ORGANIZATION

COMMANDMENTS

(ETERNAL) MARRIAGE

FAITH

MISSIONARY WORK

(PERSONAL) REVELATION

(PLAN OF) SALVATION

PRAYER

PRIESTHOOD

SECOND COMING

TEMPLES

TITHING

```
A S T N E M D N A M M O C R
V S E C O N D C O M I N G E
O R G A N I Z A T I O N O V
E I T E M P L E S C E O F E
G N O I T A V L A S W A R L
A N I N T G P R A Y E R U A
I N D O O H T S E I R P T T
R B U I L D I N G Z I O N I
R O F A I T H N A L L P E O
A B A P T I S M G O P L E N
M I S S I O N A R Y W O R K
```

WHAT IS THE DOCTRINE AND COVENANTS?

___ ___ ___ ___ ___ ___   ___ ___

___ ___ ___ ___ ___ ___   ___ ___ ___ ___

___ ___ ___   ___ ___ ___ ___ ___

Solution on page 85.

drawing from the scriptures

Each square below contains a piece of a bigger picture. Draw what you see from each box below in the empty box with matching coordinates. (An example has been done for you.) The completed pictures represent the original name of the Doctrine and Covenants.

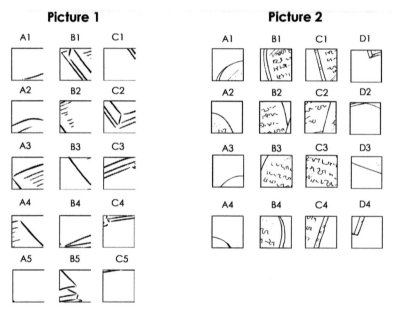

Picture 1

Picture 2

ORIGINAL NAME OF THE DOCTRINE AND COVENANTS

— — — — —

— — — — — — — — — —

Picture 1

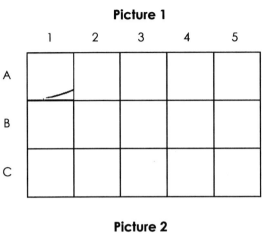

	1	2	3	4	5
A					
B					
C					

Picture 2

	1	2	3	4
A				
B				
C				
D				

Solution on page 82.

9

hangman

You'll need two or more players to play this game of hangman. Select one player to be the scribe, and the other player(s) will guess the phrase below. The scribe should look on page 81 to find the solution to the puzzle below.

LETTERS GUESSED

THE AUTHOR OF THE
DOCTRINE AND COVENANTS

___ ___ ___ ___ ___

___ ___ ___ ___ ___ ___ ___

people and

places

word search

PEOPLE

Below is a list of some of the people mentioned in the Doctrine and Covenants. Find them in the word search to the right, but be aware that the first and last names do not appear on the same line. Names can appear horizontally, vertically, diagonally, and backward. An example has been done for you.

MARTIN HARRIS

OLIVER COWDERY

HYRUM SMITH

JOSEPH KNIGHT

DAVID WHITMER

HIRAM PAGE

ZIBA PETERSON

ORSON PRATT

ORSON HYDE

EZRA THAYRE

M	A	R	T	I	N	A	E	Y	N	D	I	V	A	D
A	B	I	Z	O	H	I	R	A	M	W	F	O	M	E
P	U	M	P	G	A	Z	G	D	P	H	X	W	B	P
E	H	V	B	L	R	A	T	N	A	I	A	R	Z	E
T	C	X	C	U	R	Z	S	Y	G	T	T	C	X	D
E	Y	Q	O	L	I	V	E	R	E	M	H	Q	A	A
R	T	B	C	A	S	T	C	W	L	E	A	V	U	E
S	D	D	J	F	H	O	T	Q	H	R	Y	R	P	D
O	S	I	R	E	W	R	K	T	R	C	R	R	T	Y
N	F	E	S	D	O	T	I	K	T	E	E	F	O	H
K	I	E	E	B	S	M	T	G	H	L	P	K	G	N
L	X	R	W	A	S	A	T	F	G	D	N	U	O	O
H	Y	R	U	M	B	V	A	H	I	H	I	S	I	G
J	B	L	A	W	H	R	R	I	N	L	R	M	O	V
K	D	O	F	C	G	T	P	L	K	O	Z	J	Y	N
M	Q	H	O	R	S	O	N	J	H	P	E	S	O	J

Solution on page 85.

13

word search

PLACES

Below is a list of some of the cities and counties where the revelations found in the Doctrine and Covenants were received. Find them in the word search to the right. The name of the states have been provided just for your information. Don't search for them in the puzzle.

ILLINOIS
NAUVOO
RASMUS

MASSACHUSETTS
SALEM

MISSOURI
JACKSON COUNTY
INDEPENDENCE
FISHING RIVER
FAR WEST
SPRING HILL
CLAY COUNTY

NEBRASKA
WINTER QUARTERS

NEW YORK
MANCHESTER
FAYETTE
PERRYSBURG

OHIO
KIRTLAND
THOMPSON
ORANGE
HIRAM
AMHERST

PENNSYLVANIA
HARMONY

UTAH
SALT LAKE CITY

J	A	C	K	S	O	N	C	O	U	N	T	Y	M	W
L	D	N	A	L	T	R	I	K	A	H	H	T	A	I
P	E	R	R	Y	S	B	U	R	G	T	A	N	N	N
X	A	E	T	F	W	P	V	C	B	U	R	U	C	T
I	M	V	H	A	S	O	Q	I	H	A	M	O	H	E
L	H	I	I	Y	M	E	G	N	A	R	O	C	E	R
L	E	R	R	E	K	B	R	J	X	V	N	Y	S	Q
I	R	G	A	T	T	C	X	S	U	H	Y	A	T	U
H	S	N	M	T	O	A	U	A	Z	W	I	L	E	A
G	T	I	O	E	S	M	N	X	V	T	H	C	R	R
N	D	H	U	F	S	N	Z	U	W	G	R	F	I	T
I	O	S	I	A	T	H	O	M	P	S	O	N	G	E
R	Q	I	R	G	H	F	A	R	W	E	S	T	A	R
P	M	F	Y	T	I	C	E	K	A	L	T	L	A	S
S	R	G	A	M	M	E	L	A	S	R	O	U	I	G
D	W	X	E	C	N	E	D	N	E	P	E	D	N	I

Solution on page 86.

word search

TWELVE APOSTLES

Below is the names of the original Twelve Apostles called in this dispensation. Search for their last names in the puzzle to the right. Then find the last names of the latter-day Twelve Apostles. The names of the current apostles are not listed, so this will be an extra challenge.

THOMAS B. MARSH	PARLEY P. PRATT
DAVID W. PATTEN	LUKE S. JOHNSON
BRIGHAM YOUNG	WILLIAM SMITH
HEBER C. KIMBALL	ORSON PRATT
ORSON HYDE	JOHN E. BOYNTON
WILLIAM E. MCLELLIN	LYMAN E. JOHNSON

```
P  A  G  D  R  A  L  L  A  B  D  R  D  I  S
A  R  S  E  L  A  H  P  S  O  B  F  I  M  C
T  A  A  J  B  C  T  R  B  P  R  M  I  J  O
T  H  N  T  M  T  P  A  R  E  C  T  L  A  T
E  K  I  N  T  R  A  T  O  R  H  T  K  I  T
N  L  L  E  S  B  E  T  D  R  U  S  O  F  E
V  Y  H  L  U  S  Q  L  C  Y  N  S  V  K  D
N  O  T  S  H  O  L  L  A  N  D  O  E  K  Y
O  U  R  O  K  D  L  O  B  M  M  A  R  S  H
S  N  I  N  X  A  R  A  N  D  E  B  L  M  H
N  G  W  E  B  Z  J  O  H  N  S  O  N  K  Q
H  Z  U  M  R  A  Z  E  O  A  O  N  P  O  N
O  F  I  E  B  O  Y  N  T  O  N  D  A  O  L
J  K  W  A  V  T  G  N  I  L  L  E  L  C  M
A  K  L  S  P  A  C  K  E  R  G  N  F  L  P
C  H  R  I  S  T  O  F  F  E  R  S  O  N  A
```

Solution on page 86.

17

maze

Help Oliver Cowdery find his way to Joseph Smith's house so he can work as a scribe for Joseph.

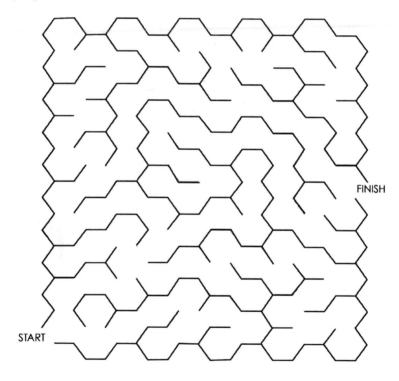

START

FINISH

Solution on page 82.

building zion

hangman

You'll need two or more players to play this game of hangman. Select one player to be the scribe, and the other player(s) will guess the phrase below. The scribe should look on page 81 to find the solution to the puzzle below.

The scribe should look on page 81 to find the solution to the puzzle below.

LETTERS GUESSED

PLACE THAT IS REFERRED TO AS "ZION" IN MANY REVELATIONS

__ __ __ __ __ __

__ __ __ __ __ __

maze

Help the Saints find their way to Zion.

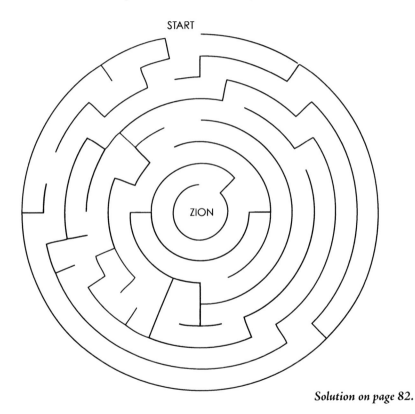

START

ZION

Solution on page 82.

pioneer picture match

Find the two pictures below and on the next page that are exactly the same. *Solution on page 83.*

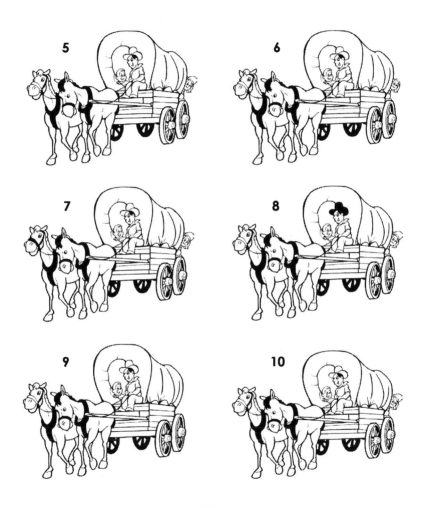

word search

TRIBULATION

Below is a list of some of the trials the early Saints experienced while striving to build Zion. Search for them in the word search on the following page. Then read the remaining letters in the grid, from left to right, to reveal what the Lord had to say about trials.

BETRAYAL

DEATH

DOUBT

FATIGUE

FEAR

FIRE

GRIEF

HARDSHIP

HUNGER

IMPRISONMENT

LOSS OF LOVED ONES

PAIN

POVERTY

ROBBBERY

SICKNESS

SORROW

THIRST

THREATS

```
F  T  N  E  M  N  O  S  I  R  P  M  I  O  R
A  F  T  E  R  M  P  A  I  N  U  C  H  T  R
I  B  B  U  L  A  T  I  O  N  C  O  M  E  T
H  E  E  E  U  G  I  T  A  F  B  L  S  E  S
P  S  T  S  I  N  G  S  W  E  H  E  O  Y  T
O  R  R  E  F  O  R  E  T  A  H  E  R  R  A
V  D  A  A  Y  C  O  M  E  R  T  F  R  E  E
E  H  Y  T  H  I  R  S  T  T  H  E  O  B  R
R  A  A  T  Y  E  S  S  H  A  L  I  W  B  H
T  L  L  B  E  C  S  R  O  W  N  R  E  O  T
Y  D  W  I  D  E  A  T  H  U  N  G  E  R  T
H  M  U  C  N  H  G  L  T  O  R  Y  T  H  E
H  O  U  K  R  I  S  B  N  O  T  Y  E  T  B
U  T  C  I  S  N  U  I  G  H  F  I  R  E  A
T  I  H  A  N  O  D  H  A  R  D  S  H  I  P
S  E  N  O  D  E  V  O  L  F  O  S  S  O  L
```

Solution on page 86.

missionary work

crossword puzzle

D&C 4

Complete the crossword puzzle to the right by filling in the missing words from the verses below. For example, 2A in the verse below is the missing word that goes in 2 across, 21D is 21 down, and so forth.

1 Now behold, a (**8D**) work is about to come forth among the children of men.

2 Therefore, O ye that (**10D**) in the (**17A**) of God, see that ye serve him with all your (**18A**), (**12A**), (**9A**) and (**4D**), that ye may stand blameless before God at the last day.

3 Therefore, if ye have (**5A**) to serve God ye are (**2D**) to the work;

4 For behold the field is (**7D**) already to (**13A**); and lo, he that thrusteth in his (**4A**) with his might, the same layeth up in store that he (**11D**) not, but bringeth (**6D**) to his soul;

5 And faith, hope, charity and (**15D**), with an eye (**3A**) to the glory of God, qualify him for the work.

6 Remember (**1D**), virtue, knowledge, temperance, patience, brotherly kindness, godliness, (**2A**), humility, diligence.

7 (**14A**), and ye shall receive; (**16A**), and it shall be opened unto you. Amen.

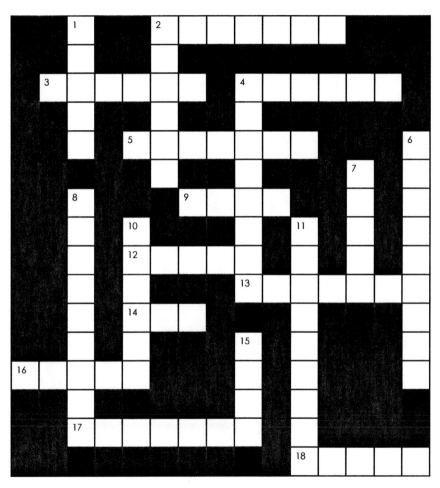

29

Solution on page 80.

scripture codes

Using the key below, decode the scripture on the following page. Then unscramble the circled letters to complete the phrase below.

A = ⬚ L = ✪ W = ♥ 5 = ◎
B = ✪ M = ⇨ X = ○ 6 = ◻
C = ☆ N = ◁ Y = ◉ 7 = ✳
D = ☐ O = ➡ Z = ☆ 8 = ❖
E = ★ P = ◀ 0 = ● 9 = ◆
F = ⊞ Q = ♡ 1 = ♣
G = ✿ R = ◙ 2 = ◻
H = ⊡ S = ♥ 3 = ⬤
I = ▣ T = ▶ 4 = 🍎
J = ✭ U = ◪
K = ✩ V = ⊡

THIS REVELATION WAS GIVEN TO JOSEPH SMITH, OLIVER

COWDERY, AND DAVID __ __ __ __ __ __ __.

(D&C ♣❖:♣●)

Solution on page 85.

crossword puzzle

D&C 11

Complete the crossword puzzle to the right by filling in the missing words from the verses below. For example, 2A in the verse below is the missing word that goes in 2 across, 21D is 21 down, and so forth.

15 Behold, I command you that you need not suppose that you are called to (**8A**) until you are called.

16 (**12A**) a little longer, until you shall have my word, my rock, my church, and my gospel, that you may know of a surety my (**5A**).

17 And then, behold, according to your desires, yea, even according to your (**4D**) shall it be done unto you.

18 Keep my (**14A**); hold your peace; appeal unto my Spirit;

19 Yea, cleave unto me with all your (**6A**), that you may assist in bringing to (**10D**) those things of which has been spoken—yea, the (**16A**) of my work; be (**11A**) until you shall accomplish it.

20 Behold, this is your (**1D**), to keep my commandments, yea, with all your might, mind and (**2D**).

21 Seek not to (**13D**) my word, but first seek to (**15D**) my word, and then shall your (**9A**) be loosed; then, if you desire, you shall have my (**17A**) and my word, yea, the power of God unto the convincing of men.

22 But now hold your peace; (**7D**) my (**18A**) which hath gone forth among the children of men, and also study my word which shall come forth among the children of men, or that which is now translating, yea, until you have obtained all which I shall grant unto the children of men in this (**3D**), and then shall all things be added thereto.

Solution on page 80.

scripture chase

D&C 96:5

This scripture chase is different from the ones you're used to. Instead of searching for scriptures in the Doctrine and Covenants, you'll search for a scripture in the grid on the following page. Begin at the circled letter and draw a line through each letter of the word as you find it. Words read forward, backward, up, and down, but not diagonally. The first letter of each word is in bold. Don't skip any letters. Every letter in the grid will be used. Use the scripture below to find out which word to search for next.

FOR BEHOLD, VERILY I SAY UNTO YOU, THIS IS THE MOST EXPEDIENT IN ME, THAT MY WORD SHOULD GO FORTH UNTO THE CHILDREN OF MEN, FOR THE PURPOSE OF SUBDUING THE HEARTS OF THE CHILDREN OF MEN FOR YOUR GOOD.

```
P  E  H  A  T  M  Y  D  R  E  N  O  F
X  D  T  D  R  O  W  L  S  O  U  P  M
E  I  E  S  T  O  H  I  E  P  R  E  E
T  E  M  H  N  T  C  F  O  D  T  H  N
S  N  N  O  U  H  E  S  O  O  R  O  F
O  T  I  U  H  T  R  U  G  O  Y  F  N
M  E  H  L  D  G  O  B  R  U  R  O  E
O  Y  T  S  I  O  F  D  E  N  O  F  M
T  O  H  I  S  I  R  U  R  D  L  S  T
N  U  T  I  Y  L  E  I  C  H  I  O  R
U  Y  A  S  H  O  V  N  E  H  T  F  A
F  O  R  B  E  L  D  G  T  H  E  H  E
```

Solution on page 84.

word search

D&C 42:11–14

Unscramble the words below. Then fill in the blanks below and search for the missing words in the word search on the next page.

CRPAEH   OSPLEG   ATECIHNGS

CRCHUH   BBIEL   AFITH

LDEERS   VEONACNST   STPIRI

11 Again I say unto you, that it shall not be given to any one to go forth to

_____ my gospel, or to build up my church, except he be ordained by some one who has authority, and it is known to the _____ that he has authority and has been regularly ordained by the heads of the church.

12 And again, the _____, priests and teachers of this church shall teach the principles of my _____, which are in the _____ and the Book of Mormon, in the which is the fulness of the gospel.

13 And they shall observe the _____ and church articles to do them, and these shall be their _____, as they shall be directed by the Spirit.

14 And the Spirit shall be given unto you by the prayer of _____; and if ye receive not the _____ ye shall not teach.

```
F I O I I Y X S S Y Y L N G Q
V S M W V Y T R T B F W L H R
M E Q J O A E N E V M G U F E
A P G S F D G P A Y X U D J U
X D P E L F Z X C C G C F Y D
A P R E N H B N H O D H A X Q
P D G F I P R H I V Q U I V B
U D U P X H J S N E K R T Y E
G Z Y T R J G J G N S C H E C
S G D K T E Y K S A P H G J V
U M G B I W A J B N I Y L W C
A B I B L E L C U T R X I Q A
J G L E E N B S H S I Q I Q K
G R N Q C P S D R W T O W Y S
O Q Y C G Z G O S P E L A B X
```

Solution on page 86.

crossword puzzle

D&C 31

Complete the crossword puzzle to the right by filling in the missing words from the verses below. For example, 2A in the verse below is the missing word that goes in 2 across, 21D is 21 down, and so forth.

3 Lift up your heart and (**14A**), for the hour of your mission is come; and your tongue shall be loosed, and you shall declare glad tidings of great joy unto this generation.

4 You shall declare the things which have been revealed to my servant, Joseph Smith, Jun. You shall begin to (**13D**) from this time forth, yea, to reap in the (**11A**) which is white already to be burned.

5 Therefore, thrust in your (**7D**) with all your soul, and your sins are forgiven you, and you shall be laden with (**6A**) upon your back, for the (**4A**) is worthy of his hire. Wherefore, your family shall live.

6 Behold, verily I say unto you, go from them only for a little time, and (**12D**) my word, and I will prepare a place for them.

7 Yea, I will open the (**15A**) of the people, and they will receive you. And I will

establish a (**9A**) by your hand;

8 And you shall (**16A**) them and prepare them against the time when they shall be gathered.

9 Be patient in (**8D**), revile not against those that revile. Govern your house in meekness, and be steadfast.

10 Behold, I say unto you that you shall be a (**1D**) unto the church, but not unto the world, for they will not receive you.

11 Go your way whithersoever I will, and it shall be given you by the (**10D**) what you shall do and whither you shall go.

12 Pray (**2D**), lest you enter into temptation and lose your (**5D**).

13 Be (**3A**) unto the end, and lo, I am with you. These words are not of man nor of men, but of me, even Jesus Christ, your Redeemer, by the will of the Father. Amen.

Solution on page 81.

hangman

You'll need two or more players to play this game of hangman. Select one player to be the scribe, and the other player(s) will guess the phrase below. The scribe should look on page 81 to find the solution to the puzzle below.

LETTERS GUESSED

HOW MISSIONARIES
SHOULD TEACH

___ ___ ___

___ ___

___ ___ ___

maze

Help the missionaries find their way back home to their families.

START

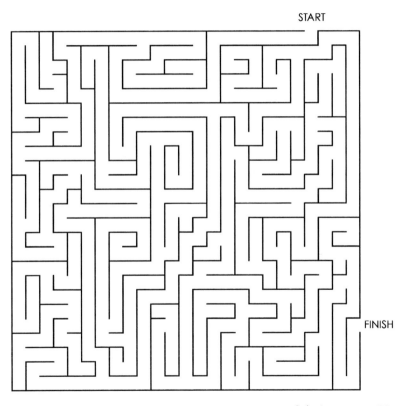

FINISH

Solution on page 82.

hangman

You'll need two or more players to play this game of hangman. Select one player to be the scribe, and the other player(s) will guess the phrase below. The scribe should look on page 81 to find the solution to the puzzle below.

LETTERS GUESSED

WITH WHAT YOU
SHOULD SERVE

_ _ _   _ _ _ _

_ _ _ _ _,

_ _ _ _ _,

_ _ _ _,   _ _ _

_ _ _ _ _ _ _

prayer

scripture codes

Using the key below, decode the scripture on the following page. Then unscramble the circled letters to complete the phrase below.

A = 🌼   K = ⟨   U = 😊   3 = ●

B = ◎   L = ◈   V = ❈   4 = 🍎

C = ◯   M = ☺   W = ✿   5 = ◉

D = ◉   N = ◉   X = ◎   6 = ☐

E = ❀   O = ✦   Y = ❀   7 = ✳

F = ❁   P = ⊖   Z = ◑   8 = ❖

G = ◌   Q = ◯   9 = ◆

H = ⊞   R = ✿   0 = ●

I = ～   S = ✿   1 = ♣

J = ♀   T = ⊖   2 = ☐

IN THIS SECTION, THE LORD TELLS JOSEPH OF THE ALTERATIONS MADE TO THE LOST 116 PAGES THAT WERE IN THE POSSESSION OF

__ __ __ __ I __   __ __ __ __ __ __.

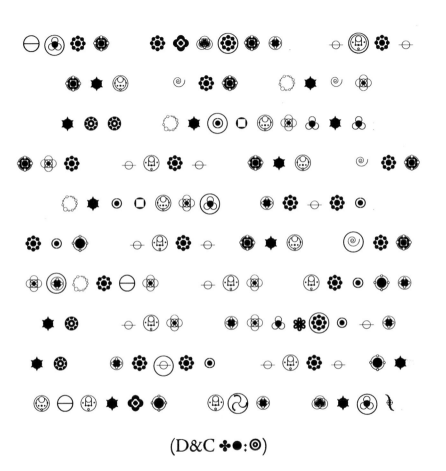

(D&C ♣●:◎)

Solution on page 85.

drawing from the scriptures

Each square below contains a piece of a bigger picture. Draw what you see from each box below in the empty box with matching coordinates. (An example has been done for you.) The completed picture represents something we must do daily.

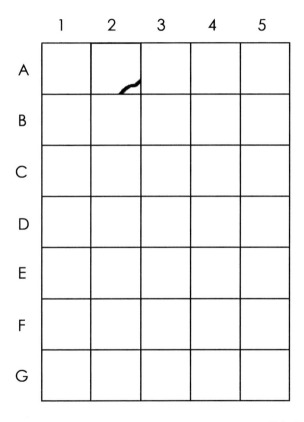

Solution on page 82.

scripture chase

D&C 8:2

This scripture chase is different from the ones you're used to. Instead of searching for scriptures in the Doctrine and Covenants, you'll search for a scripture in the grid on the following page. Begin at the circled letter and draw a line through each letter of the word as you find it. Words read forward, backward, up, and down, but not diagonally. The first letter of each word is in bold. Don't skip any letters. Every letter in the grid will be used. Use the scripture below to find out which word to search for next.

I WILL TELL YOU IN YOUR MIND AND IN YOUR HEART, BY THE HOLY GHOST, WHICH SHALL COME UPON YOU AND WHICH SHALL DWELL IN YOUR HEART.

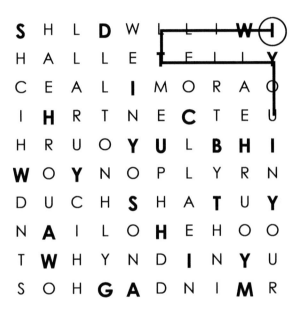

Solution on page 84.

commandments

word search

D&C 25

The Lord commanded Emma Smith to compile a hymnbook. Below is a list of some of the hymns that appeared in the first hymnbook. In the puzzle to the right, search for the words that are in bold. Then read the remaning letters in the puzzle, from left to right, to reveal what the Lord said about hymns.

KNOW THEN THAT **EVERY SOUL IS FREE**

REDEEMER OF ISRAEL

SEE **ALL CREATION** JOIN

TO HIM THAT **MADE THE WORLD**

NOW LET US REJOICE

THE **HAPPY DAY** HAS ROLLED ON

HOW FIRM **A FOUNDATION**

THE SPIRIT OF GOD **LIKE A FIRE** IS BURNING

NOW WE'LL SING WITH **ONE ACCORD**

LET ZION IN HER **BEAUTY** RISE

ADAM-ONDI-**AHMAN**

WE'RE **NOT ASHAMED** TO OWN OUR LORD

COME ALL YE **SAINTS** WHO DWELL ON EARTH

GUIDE US, O THOU GREAT **JEHOVAH**

HE DIED! THE GREAT **REDEEMER** DIED

JOY TO THE WORLD

JESUS, MIGHTY **KING IN ZION**

HOW **PLEASANT** 'TIS TO SEE

THE LORD INTO HIS **GARDEN** COMES

```
F  O  J  E  H  O  V  A  H  R  M  K  D  M  E  R
Y  S  R  O  U  L  H  D  E  L  I  R  A  C  E  D
I  G  E  H  T  M  E  T  H  N  O  D  I  D  I  L
N  T  D  H  A  E  S  O  G  C  E  O  E  H  N  R
G  P  E  N  O  F  T  I  C  T  J  E  A  D  H  O
L  L  E  E  H  E  N  A  H  E  M  P  A  E  R  W
I  E  M  T  T  Z  E  E  R  E  P  S  H  M  E  E
K  A  E  S  I  N  W  S  R  Y  B  T  O  A  N  H
E  S  R  O  O  O  U  O  D  G  E  N  O  H  F  T
A  A  N  T  R  T  F  A  H  E  A  I  R  S  I  O
F  N  G  L  E  I  Y  H  T  E  U  A  O  A  U  T
I  T  D  L  S  S  I  S  A  P  T  S  R  T  A  Y
R  Y  W  R  N  E  D  R  A  G  Y  E  R  O  U  O
E  O  A  F  O  U  N  D  A  T  I  O  N  N  N  J
N  E  E  R  F  S  I  L  U  O  S  Y  R  E  V  E
L  T  O  A  L  L  C  R  E  A  T  I  O  N  M  E
```

Solution on page 87.

missing vowels

BLESSINGS FROM THE WORD OF WISDOM

A list of blessings from followig the Word of Wisdom (D&C 89:18–21) appears on the following page. However, all of the vowels are missing. Fill in the vowels that will complete each word. The missing vowels are below.

A A A A A A A A A A A

E E E E E E E E E E E E

I I I I I   O O O O O O O O   U U

1. H _ _ L T H   _ N   T H _

   N _ V _ L

2. M _ R R _ W   _ N   T H _

   B _ N _ S

3. W _ S D _ M

4. T R _ _ S _ R _ S   _ F

   K N _ W L _ D G _

5. R _ N   _ N D   N _ T   B _

   W _ _ R Y

6. W _ L K   _ N D   N _ T   F _ _ N T

7. D _ S T R _ Y _ N G   _ N G _ L

   S H _ L L   P _ S S

Solution on page 84.

drawing from the scriptures

D&C 132

Each square below contains a piece of a bigger picture. Draw what you see from each box below in the empty box with matching coordinates. (An example has been done for you.) The completed picture represents an ordinance we must receive in order to earn the highest degree in the celestial kingdom.

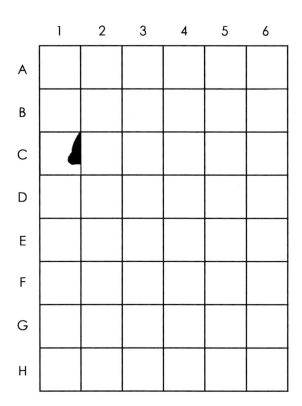

THE ORDINANCE WE MUST RECEIVE IN ORDER TO REACH
THE HIGHEST DEGREE IN THE CELESTIAL KINGDOM

___ ___ ___ ___ ___ ___ ___

___ ___ ___ ___ ___ ___ ___

Solution on page 82.

scripture chase

D&C 82:10

This scripture chase is different from the ones you're used to. Instead of searching for scriptures in the Doctrine and Covenants, you'll search for a scripture in the grid below. Begin at the circled letter and draw a line through each letter of the word as you find it. Words read forward, backward, up, and down, but not diagonally. The first letter of each word is in bold. Don't skip any letters. Every letter in the grid will be used. Use the scripture below to find out which word to search for next.

I, THE LORD, AM ABOUND WHEN YE DO WHAT I SAY;
BUT WHEN YE DO NOT WHAT I SAY, YE HAVE NO
PROMISE.

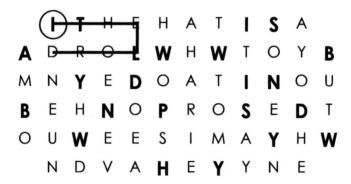

Solution on page 84.

hangman

You'll need two or more players to play this game of hangman. Select one player to be the scribe, and the other player(s) will guess the phrase below. The scribe should look on page 81 to find the solution to the puzzle below.

LETTERS GUESSED

WHAT WE MUST DO WITH
OUR SINS IN ORDER TO
TRULY REPENT

___ ___ ___ ___ ___ ___ ___

___ ___ ___

___ ___ ___ ___ ___ ___ ___

plan of salvation

missing vowels

REQUIREMENTS FOR BAPTISM—D&C 20:37

On the following page you will find a list of the requirements for baptism. However, all of the vowels are missing. Fill in the vowels that will complete each word. The missing vowels are below.

A A A A

E E E E E E E E E E E E E E E E E E E E E E

I I I I I I I I I I I I I I I

O O O O O O O O O

U U

1 . H __ M __ L __ T Y

2 . D __ S __ R __

3 . B R __ K __ N   H __ __ R T

4 . C __ N T R __ T __   S P __ R __ T

5 . R __ P __ N T __ N C __

6 . W __ L L __ N G N __ S S   T __   T __ K __

   __ P __ N   T H __   N __ M __   __ F

   C H R __ S T

7 . D __ T __ R M __ N __ T __ __ N   T __

   S __ R V __   H __ M   T __

   T H __   __ N D

8 . R __ C __ __ V __   T H __   S P __ R __ T

   __ F   C H R __ S T

Solution on page 83.

secret code

D&C 50:23–24

In D&C 50:23–24 we learn that all things that are good come from God. Ue the code below to spell the words on the next page. Then circle the words that describe things that come from God. Unscramble the first letter of each circled word to discover what will help you know if something is from God.

A = ◎
B = ○
C = ◖
D = ◉
E = ◉
F = ❄
G = ❆
H = ⁙
I = ⚶
J = ⁘
K = ⛊
L = ▦
M = ⊕
N = ✴
O = ✤
P = ⛌
Q = ⚙
R = ✳
S = ✸
T = ◉
U = ◉
V = ✿
W = ✤
X = ◉
Y = ❋
Z = ✸

Now unscramble the first letter of each circled word to discover what will help you know if something is from God.

___ ___ ___ Y ___ ___ O ___ ___

Solution on page 83.

crossword puzzle

D&C 137

Complete the crossword puzzle to the right by filling in the missing words from the verses below. For example, 2A in the verse below is the missing word that goes in 2 across, 21D is 21 down, and so forth.

1 The (**3D**) were opened upon us, and I beheld the (**4A**) kingdom of God, and the glory thereof, whether in the body or out I cannot tell.

2 I saw the transcendent beauty of the gate through which the (**14A**) of that kingdom will enter, which was like unto circling flames of fire;

3 Also the blazing (**13A**) of God, whereon was seated the (**1D**) and the (**15D**).

4 I saw the beautiful streets of that kingdom, which had the appearance of being paved with (**11A**).

5 I saw Father Adam and (**9D**); and my father and my mother; my brother (**12A**), that has long since slept;

6 And marveled how it was that he had obtained an (**5D**) in that kingdom, seeing that he had departed this life before the Lord had set his hand to gather Israel the second time, and had not been (**10D**) for the remission of sins.

7 Thus came the voice of the Lord unto me, saying: All who have died without a (**16A**) of this gospel, who would have (**6A**) it if they had been permitted to tarry, shall be heirs of the celestial kingdom of God;

8 Also all that shall die henceforth without a knowledge of it, who would have received it with all their (**2D**), shall be heirs of that kingdom;

9 For I, the Lord, will (**8D**) all men according to their works, according to the desire of their hearts.

10 And I also beheld that all (**7D**) who die before they arrive at the years of accountability are saved in the celestial kingdom of heaven.

67

Solution on page 81.

missing letters

THE RESTORATION OF PRIESTHOOD KEYS

Below are the names of seven prophets who appeared to Joseph Smith to pass on sacred priesthood keys. However, every other letter is missing. Fill in the missing letters that will complete each word. The missing letters are below. *Solution on page 83.*

A   E E E E E   H H H   I   J J J J   L

M   O   S S S   T T

1 . M __ S __ S   (GATHERING OF ISRAEL)

2 . __ A __ E __   (MELCHIZEDEK PRIESTHOOD)

3 . P __ T __ R   (MELCHIZEDEK PRIESTHOOD)

4 . __ O __ N __ H __ B __ P __ I __ T   (AARONIC PRIESTHOOD)

5 . __ O __ N   (MELCHIZEDEK PRIESTHOOD)

6 . E __ I __ A __   (SEALING POWER OF THE PRIESTHOOD)

7 . __ L __ A __   (COMMITTED THE DISPENSATION OF THE GOSPEL OF
            ABRAHAM))

hangman

You'll need two or more players to play this game of hangman. Select one player to be the scribe, and the other player(s) will guess the phrase below. The scribe should look on page 81 to find the solution to the puzzle below.

LETTERS GUESSED

A TEMPLE ORDINANCE

___ ___ ___ ___ ___ ___ ___

___ ___ ___ ___ ___ ___

___ ___ ___ ___ ___

crossword puzzle

D&C 6

Complete the crossword puzzle to the right by filling in the missing words from the verses below. For example, 2A in the verse below is the missing word that goes in 2 across, 21D is 21 down, and so forth.

7 Seek not for (**1A**) but for (**10D**), and behold, the mysteries of God shall be unfolded unto you, and then shall you be made rich. Behold, he that hath (**8D**) life is rich.

8 Verily, verily, I say unto you, even as you desire of me so it shall be unto you; and if you desire, you shall be the means of doing much good in this generation.

9 Say nothing but (**11A**) unto this generation; keep my (**2D**), and assist to bring forth my work, according to my commandments, and you shall be (**7A**).

10 Behold thou hast a (**12D**), and blessed art thou because of thy gift. Remember it is (**6A**) and cometh from above—

11 And if thou wilt inquire, thou shalt know (**4A**) which are great and marvelous; therefore thou shalt exercise thy gift, that thou mayest find out mysteries, that thou mayest bring many to the knowledge of the (**9D**), yea, convince them of the error of their ways.

12 Make not thy gift known unto any save it be those who are of thy (**3D**). Trifle not with sacred things.

13 If thou wilt do good, yea, and hold out (**14A**) to the end, thou shalt be saved in the (**13A**) of God, which is the greatest of all the gifts of God; for there is no gift greater than the gift of (**5D**).

Solution on page 81.

everything else

hangman

You'll need two or more players to play this game of hangman. Select one player to be the scribe, and the other player(s) will guess the phrase on the following page. The scribe should look on page 81 to find the solution to the puzzle below.

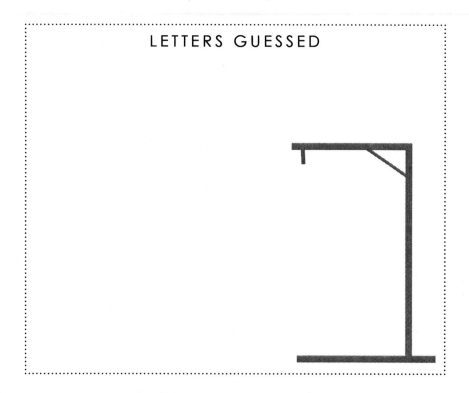

LETTERS GUESSED

___ ___ ___ ___ ___   ___ ___   ___ ___,

___ ___ ___   ___ ___ ___ ___ ___ ___

___ ___   ___ ___   ___ ___ ___ ___ ___;

___ ___ ___ ___   ___ ___   ___ ___ ___

___ ___ ___ ___ ___ ___ ___

___ ___   ___ ___   ___ ___ ___ ___ ___ ___,

___ ___ ___   ___ ___ ___

___ ___ ___ ___ ___   ___ ___ ___ ___

___ ___ ___ ___ ___   ___ ___   ___ ___.

scripture chase

D&C 3:2

This scripture chase is different from the ones you're used to. Instead of searching for scriptures in the Doctrine and Covenants, you'll search for a scripture in the grid on the following page. Begin at the circled letter and draw a line through each letter of the word as you find it. Words read forward, backward, up, and down, but not diagonally. The first letter of each word is in bold. Don't skip any letters. Every letter in the grid will be used. Use the scripture below to find out which word to search for next.

GOD DOTH NOT WALK IN CROOKED PATHS, NEITHER DOTH HE TURN TO THE RIGHT HAND NOR TO THE LEFT, NEITHER DOTH HE VARY FROM THAT WHICH HE HATH SAID, THEREFORE HIS PATHS ARE STRAIGHT, AND HIS COURSE IS ONE ETERNAL ROUND.

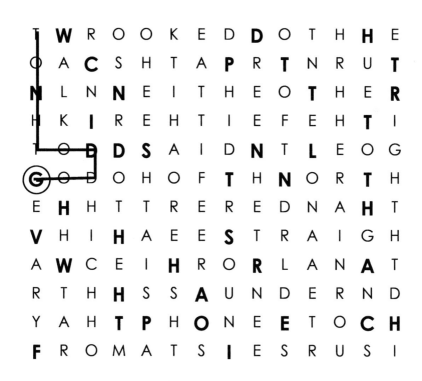

Solution on page 84.

missing letters

GIFTS OF THE SPIRIT—D&C 46

On the following page is a list of the gifts of the spirit found in D&C 46. However, every other letter is missing. Fill in the missing letters that will complete each word. The missing letters are below.

A   C   D   E E E E E E E E

F F F   G G G   H

I I I I I I   L   M M   N N N N N N

O O O O O   P P P   R R R

S S S S   T T   W W   Y

1. __ I __ D __ M

2. K __ O __ L __ D __ E

3. __ A __ T __

4. H __ A __ I __ G

5. __ E __ F __ R __ I __ G

   __ I __ A __ L __ S

6. P __ O __ H __ C __

7. __ I __ C __ R __ I __ G   __ F

   __ P __ R __ T __

8. G __ F __   O __   T __ N __ U __ S

9. I __ T __ R __ R __ T __ T __ O __   O __

   T __ N __ U __ S

Solution on page 83.

answer key

crossword puzzle

Page 3
ACROSS
3. LEG
6. FOURTEEN
8. JOSEPH SMITH SR.
12. PALMYRA
14. GROVE
15. MORONI
16. PERSONAGES

DOWN
1. DECEMBER
2. VERMONT
4. NONE
5. JAMES
7. CHURCH
9. EMMA HALE
10. SPRING
11. SEVEN
13. APRIL

Page 5
ACROSS
4. COMMANDMENTS
5. EARTH
6. BLOOD
8. SLAIN
12. GREAT
13. SALVATION
15. CITY
16. TWENTY
18. THOUSANDS

DOWN
1. CONTINENTS
2. ANOINTED
3. SEALED
7. DIVIDED
9. EVERLASTING
10. JESUS
11. PROPHET
12. GOD
14. HYRUM
17. GOD

Page 29
ACROSS
2. CHARITY
3. SINGLE
4. SICKLE
5. DESIRES
9. MIND
12. MIGHT
13. HARVEST
14. ASK
16. KNOCK
17. SERVICE
18. HEART

DOWN
1. FAITH
2. CALLED
4. STRENGTH
6. JESUS
7. WHITE
8. MARVELOUS
10. EMBARK
11. PERISHETH
15. LOVE

Page 33
ACROSS
5. DOCTRINE
6. HEART
8. PREACH
9. TONGUE
11. PATIENT
12. WAIT
14. COMMAND-MENTS
16. TRANSLATION
17. SPIRIT
18. WORD

DOWN
1. WORK
2. STRENGTH
3. GENERATION
4. FAITH
7. STUDY
10. LIGHT
13. DECLARE
15. OBTAIN

crossword puzzle (continued)

Page 39

ACROSS
3. FAITHFUL
4. LABORER
6. SHEAVES
9. CHURCH
11. FIELD
14. REJOICE
15. HEARTS
16. STRENGTHEN

DOWN
1. PHYSICIAN
2. ALWAYS
5. REWARD
7. SICKLE
8. AFFLICTIONS
10. COMFORTER
12. DECLARE
13. PREACH

Page 67

ACROSS
4. CELESTIAL
6. RECEIVED
11. GOLD
12. ALVIN
13. THRONE
14. HEIRS
16. KNOWLEDGE

DOWN
1. FATHER
2. HEARTS
3. HEAVENS
5. INHERITANCE
7. CHILDREN
8. JUDGE
9. ABRAHAM
10. BAPTIZED
15. SON

Page 71

ACROSS
1. RICHES
4. MYSTERIES
6. SACRED
7. BLESSED
11. REPENTANCE
13. KINGDOM
14. FAITHFUL

DOWN
2. COMMANDMENTS
3. FAITH
5. SALVATION
8. ETERNAL
9. TRUTH
10. WISDOM
12. GIFT

---

hangman

Page 10
JESUS CHRIST (D&C 1:38)

Page 20
JACKSON COUNTY
(D&C 124:51)

Page 40
TWO BY TWO (D&C 42:6)

Page 42
ALL YOUR HEART, MIGHT, MIND,
AND STRENGTH (D&C 4:2)

Page 59
CONFESS AND FORSAKE
(D&C 88:42–43)

Page 69
BAPTISM FOR THE DEAD
(D&C 128:16)

Page 75
Learn of me, and listen to my
words; walk in the meekness of
my Spirit, and you shall have
peace in me. (D&C 19:23)

drawing from the scriptures

Page 9

BOOK OF COMMANDMENTS

Page 57

ETERNAL MARRIAGE

Page 47

mazes

Page 18

Page 21

Page 41

missing letters

Page 55
HEALTH IN THE NAVEL
MARROW IN THE BONES
WISDOM
TREASURES OF KNOWLEDGE
RUN AND NOT BE WEARY
WALK AND NOT FAINT
DESTROYING ANGEL SHALL PASS

Page 63
HUMILITY
DESIRE
BROKEN HEART
CONTRITE SPIRIT
REPENTANCE
WILLINGNESS TO TAKE UPON THE NAME OF CHRIST
DETERMINATION TO SERVE HIM TO THE END
RECEIVE THE SPIRIT OF CHRIST

Page 68
1. MOSES (GATHERING OF ISRAEL)
2. JAMES (MELCHIZEDEK PRIESTHOOD)
3. PETER (MELCHIZEDEK PRIESTHOOD)
4. JOHN THE BAPTIST (AARONIC PRIESTHOOD)
5. JOHN (MELCHIZEDEK PRIESTHOOD)
6. ELIJAH (SEALING POWERS OF THE PRIESTHOOD)
7. ELIAS (COMMITTED THE DISPENSATION OF THE GOSPEL OF ABRAHAM)

Page 79
WISDOM
KNOWLEDGE
FAITH
HEALING
PERFORMING MIRACLES
PROPHECY
DISCERNING OF SPIRITS
GIFT OF TONGUES
INTERPRETATION OF TONGUES

---

pioneer picture match

Pages 22–23
Numbers 2 and 7 are the same.

---

secret code

Page 65
FIGHTING
HAPPINESS
SIN
SHARING
MISERY

DARKNESS
LYING
HYMNS
OBEDIENCE
THOUGHTFULNESS
CHEATING

DISOBEDIENCE
LOVE
GRATITUDE

HOLY GHOST

scripture chase

Page 35

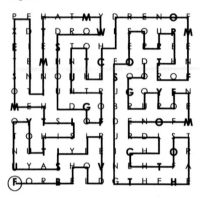

Page 49

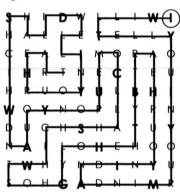

Page 58

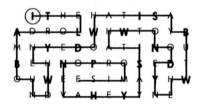

Page 77

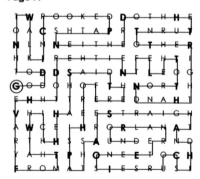

scripture code

Page 31
Remember the worth of souls is great in the sight of God. (D&C 18:10)—WHITMER

PAGE 45
Pray always, that you may come off conqueror, yea that you may conquer Satan and that you may escape the hands of the servants of Satan, that do uphold his work. (D&C 10:5)—MARTIN HARRIS

Page 49
Yea, behold, I will tell you in your mind and in your heart, by the Holy Ghost, which shall come upon you and which shall dwell in your heart. (D&C 8:2)—OLIVER COWDERY

Page 77
Therefore, fear not, little flock; do good; let earth and hell combine against you, for if ye are built upon my rock, they cannot prevail. (D&C 6:33)—HARMONY

---

word search

Page 7

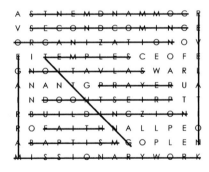

A VOICE OF WARNING UNTO ALL PEOPLE

Page 13

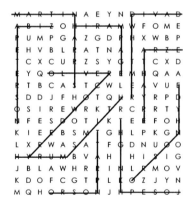

85

word search (continued)

Page 15

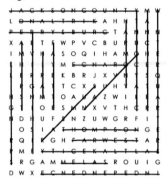

Page 17

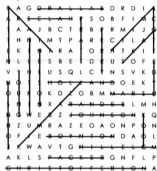

Page 25

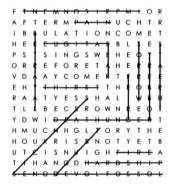

For after much tribulation come the blessings. Wherefore the day cometh that ye shall be crowned with much glory; the hour is not yet, but is nigh at hand (D&C 58:4).

Page 37

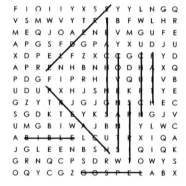

86

word search (continued)

Page 53

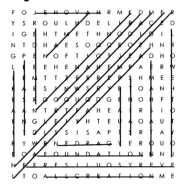

For my soul delighteth in the song of the heart; yea, the song of the righteous is a prayer unto me, and it shall be answered with a blessing upon their heads (D&C 25:12).

0 26575 51913 6